NO TIME OUT

the *Life-Story* of

GEORGE AND DOROTHY THOMAS

by

Betty M. Hockett

GEORGE FOX PRESS
600 EAST THIRD STREET • NEWBERG, OREGON 97132

To
MARGARET
who gives generous amounts of help and
encouragement to her friend, and who collects all
manner of lemons.

NO TIME OUT

The LIFE-STORY of George and Dorothy Thomas

© 1991 George Fox Press
Library of Congress Catalog Card Number: 91-072897
ISBN: 0-943701-19-8

Cover and sketches by Jannelle Loewen

Litho in U.S.A. by The Barclay Press, Newberg, Oregon

CONTENTS

1. Around and Around Goes George 1
2. Thin Ice 7
3. Here Comes the Bride 13
4. The Fiery Accident 19
5. People-eating Lions 29
6. A Change of Scenery 39
7. Beginning of A Miracle 47
8. The Merry-Go-Round 57
9. Moving Ahead 65
10. Shouting-good News 73

The Life-Story from Missions Series

FROM HERE TO THERE AND BACK AGAIN
*the life-story of Dr. Charles DeVol,
missionary to China and Taiwan.*

WHAT WILL TOMORROW BRING?
*the life-story of Ralph and Esther Choate,
missionaries to Burundi, Africa.*

DOWN A WINDING ROAD
*the life-story of Roscoe and Tina Knight,
missionaries to Bolivia, Peru, and Mexico City.*

HAPPINESS UNDER THE INDIAN TREES
*the life-story of Catherine Cattell,
missionary to India and Taiwan.*

CATCHING THEIR TALK IN A BOX
*the life-story of Joy Ridderhof,
founder of Gospel Recordings.*

MUD ON THEIR WHEELS
*the life-story of Vern and Lois Ellis,
missionaries to the Navajo Indians.*

WHISTLING BOMBS AND BUMPY TRAINS
*the life-story of Anna Nixon,
missionary to India.*

KEEPING THEM ALL IN STITCHES
*the life-story of Geraldine Custer,
missionary to Burundi, Africa.*

NO TIME OUT
*the life-story of George and Dorothy Thomas,
missionaries to Burundi and Rwanda, Africa,
and the Navajo Indians.*

*All by Betty Hockett, writer of Christian education
curriculum and stories for children.*

Chapter 1

AROUND AND AROUND GOES GEORGE

"George, don't forget I'm counting on you to help in the sawmill this morning," said Clyde Thomas that day in 1931.

"I won't, Dad," replied twelve-year-old George. "Soon as I milk the cows, I'll be out." He swallowed the last bites of pancake while his sister and four brothers jabbered about their plans.

George gulped two swallows of milk, then swiped away the white mustache with his shirt sleeve. He pushed the chair away from the table and headed out to the barn. The morning chores did not take long, and soon George hurried off across the yard.

He ran past the big stack of logs waiting beside his dad's water-powered mill located in Gates, Oregon. The big saw would eventually cut all of the logs into boards. His father had already begun to show him how to fit the boards together to create the doors and windows people ordered. Clyde often said as they worked, "Do your job the best you can."

Inside the mill that morning, George watched the stream of water trickle onto the saw to keep it cool. He reached to adjust the water flow. Suddenly, his shirt sleeve caught on a setscrew. The shaft of the saw grabbed him.

Instantly the shaft wound George up on itself, sending him around and around at the same speed as the saw. His legs thumped the wooden floor like the beat of a drum.

At the same time, George's brain began to replay unpleasant memories...trouble he had gotten into for fighting on the way home from school...hours spent in the school principal's office...bad behavior in the classroom...the candy bar he had stolen from the neighborhood store.

Around and around he went. Thud, thud! While his legs pounded, his brain raced. *If I die now, I won't go to heaven.*

It seemed forever before his father shut off the saw. The shaft turned slower...and slower...and ...slower. At last the thudding quit. George dangled over the shaft.

Clyde worked fast to untangle George's shirt sleeve and then carried him into the house. He knew from experience exactly what he had to do. As gently as he could, he felt for broken bones. "George," he explained softly, "your legs are broken in several places. I know it'll hurt, but I must straighten them out before I take you to Dr. Pemberton."

Pain attacked every part of George's body. He moaned as his father carefully worked the broken bones into place. He tried not to cry out as Clyde placed him in the back seat of the car for the fifty-mile drive to Salem.

George had never noticed so many bumps in the road. He did not remember the car jerking like this, either. At last the jolting ride ended.

Dr. Pemberton took X rays, then said, "You've done a good job of setting that boy's bones, Clyde. They're all in place. In fact, only one leg needs a cast. Soon as I put that on him, you can take George back home."

Before long, the broken legs healed, and so did the badly wrenched shoulder. New skin grew onto places rubbed raw in the go-arounds.

After that nerve-wracking-bone-breaking experience, George thought more seriously about life and what God wanted him to do. Perhaps he should be a missionary. He had met missionaries from Africa, so maybe he would go there.

Several times George started to accept Jesus as his Savior. A disturbing thought, however, always stopped him: he would have to pay back the candy he had stolen from that little store.

Finally, at home one day, George decided, *I'll do whatever the Lord shows me, even if it kills me.*

Once he had paid for the stolen candy, he discovered he could freely talk to God. At last he had peace in his conscience. He felt sure he would be a missionary to Africa someday.

Clyde and Mary Thomas and their children. Left to right – George (a college student), Mary, Allen, David, Willie.

No one suspected that the Thomas family would eventually turn out several missionaries – George, his brothers David and Willy, his father and mother, his nephew Hal, and his niece Dorothy.

* * *

Clyde and Mary Thomas and their children lived close to the Santiam River and the Cascade Mountains. Clyde, who came from a pioneer family of hunters, passed his outdoor skills on to his sons.

His 12-gauge shotgun stood nearly as tall as George. Even so, George had to use it to guard the cherry trees. Bands of wild, hungry pigeons could strip a treeful of fruit in no time at all. As the cherries ripened, George would crouch behind the old rail fence close to the cherry trees. He waited quietly while a few pigeons surveyed the situation, calling to others. As the flock swooped down for the cherries, he pulled the trigger. Sometimes he hit as many as three pigeons with one shot.

He would need these hunting skills in Africa, but of course he did not know anything about that, yet.

According to United States law at that time, young American men had to register with the government when they turned eighteen. Then, if needed, the army could draft them into service.

George obeyed the law, becoming number 241 in Washington County, Oregon. When he signed up, however, he stated, "I don't believe in war."

"In that case," the clerk of the draft board said, "we'll assign you the status of conscientious objector." This meant that if war broke out George would not have to become a soldier. Instead, he could do other important jobs to help his country.

He went on to Pacific College in Newberg, Oregon. A few days before graduation, a friend said, "I've heard of a place in Kentucky that might interest you – Kentucky Mountain Bible Institute."

The young lady then told him about the school. Something she said intrigued George. The next day he wrote a letter asking if they needed teachers there.

He could hardly wait for a reply. When it came, George exclaimed happily, "The school has hired me to teach."

Soon, he set out for KMBI, located in "Bloody Breathitt" County, famous for feuds and lawlessness. He taught in the high school for a while, then worked at other jobs at KMBI. Those next two years became the happiest of his life so far. "I know the Lord led me here," he said.

During that time, George decided for sure he should be a missionary to Africa. "I've had some doubts about it," he explained. "The Lord has made it plain to me recently that He called me even before I became a Christian." George never again doubted God's plan for his life.

One day his friends told him about a young woman named Dorothy Hughes. "She did attend school here at KMBI," they said. "Now she's going to college in Iowa. Dorothy is a lovely girl. She plans to be a missionary to Africa."

The next week George Thomas did something unusual for him: he wrote a letter to a young woman he didn't know—Dorothy Hughes.

Chapter 2

THIN ICE

A long time before Dorothy Hughes went to Iowa, she lived in the mountains of <u>Kentucky</u>. The daughter of Mackey and Rose Hughes, she grew up on a farm near <u>Cabin Creek</u>.

Just before morning recess one day, six-year-old Dorothy heard the teacher say, "Children, now you may go outside to play."

Dorothy grabbed her warm coat and hat. She jammed her arms into the coat sleeves and pulled the hat over her ears. With mittens in hand, she raced outside to the frozen creek. She did not slow down at all as her feet hit the ice. A glorious skid sent her coasting at a speed that snatched her breath.

All at once, her feet hit a patch of thin ice. Dorothy dropped into the frigid water below. She gasped, with not enough breath left to yell for help. Her arms lunged outward. She scrabbled at the jagged ice to pull herself up onto solid footing. With each grab, the ice broke into chunks.

None of the other children, or the teacher either, noticed what had happened. Only Mrs. Lyons, who lived next to the schoolhouse, saw Dorothy in trouble.

Finally, Dorothy succeeded in scrambling onto thick ice.

Mrs. Lyons, running as fast as her old, stiff legs could move, shouted, "Dorothy! Dorothy! Let me help you."

It only took a minute to lead the shivering girl to her warm house. Once inside, Mrs. Lyons quickly peeled off Dorothy's dripping clothes and wrapped her in one of her own dresses. After that, she sent for someone to come from the Hughes's household to take Dorothy home.

All her life, Dorothy shuddered whenever she remembered that fall through the thin ice.

* * *

Dorothy worked outside in the summertime, along with her seven brothers and sisters. They hoed in the garden, pulled weeds, or helped pick tomatoes for their mother to can. Mackey Hughes paid each of his children a small amount of money for helping. A few weeks before school started, the children trooped to the general store to pick out material for their school clothes.

"I feel rich," said Dorothy as she stood before the bolts of red, green, blue, yellow, and brown cloth. Some looked plain. Others bloomed with tiny flowers. A few pieces had precise lines crisscrossing into colorful plaids. It took her a long time to choose colors and designs.

Mrs. Hughes and the children attended Sunday school and church. Whenever a revival started up nearby, she made sure they all went. Dorothy loved those bumpy rides in the family wagon pulled by Molly and Daisy. She even yet remembers Molly, whose mane looked like a zebra's body with one streak of white and one of black.

Every evening Mrs. Hughes gathered the children together so each could say the Lord's Prayer. Dorothy decided one night to pray like Uncle Charley, her mother's only brother.

She arranged herself on one knee in full view of her family and some guests. Dorothy then turned her face upward and launched into a loud, full-of-authority, Uncle Charley tone, "Our Father which art in heaven, hallowed be thy name. Thy kingdom come...."

The others opened their eyes to stare at her.

"Dorothy!" Mackey Hughes rebuked from an adjoining room. "Stop that mimicking and pray right."

Dorothy never again tried to pray like Uncle Charley.

One day, a certain group of religious people in the area announced a date when Jesus would come to earth again. Dorothy's wrongdoings suddenly paraded through her mind. "That's just next month," she said. "I'm scared."

"Me too," her brother Winn admitted.

From then on, Dorothy and Winn talked of little else, though their mother did not appear concerned. The dreaded day arrived. All morning the two strolled around the yard arm-in-arm.

"I hope we won't be left behind when Jesus comes," Dorothy whispered.

"I don't want to miss going with Jesus, either," Winn answered.

"Maybe we ought to tell Him we're sorry for the bad stuff we've done," Dorothy suggested. Winn agreed.

They found a private place behind the chicken house and knelt next to a stump. Both confessed their disobedience. They admitted to having been mean in recent days. Next, they took turns asking God to forgive them. The day seemed a little less scary afterward. Even so, they still gazed at the sky every few minutes, wondering.

The rest of the day, Dorothy and Winn did everything their mother asked. They even offered to help with jobs they usually didn't like to do.

Doomsday passed and the fear that had overtaken them grew dimmer. Before long, they once again turned back to their old ways.

Sometime after Dorothy's thirteenth birthday she went to a revival meeting in the schoolhouse. Two nights before it ended, she knew God had spoken to her.

She went home and thought about it as she put on her nightgown. Crawling into bed, she remembered all the times she had disobeyed God.

The more the thoughts flicked through her mind, the worse she felt. The clock chimed the hours away as Dorothy lay wide awake, tossing from one side to the other.

Finally, she told God, *If you let me go back to another service, I'll confess my sins and let You be my Savior.*

She kept her promise at the meeting the next night, and God forgave her sin. Dorothy said to God two weeks later, "For the rest of my life I'll do whatever you want me to."

When she finished grade school, her parents arranged for her to attend high school at Kentucky Mountain Bible Institute. One day, God spoke to Dorothy again. He said, *I want you to be a missionary to Africa.*

She gladly accepted God's plans and set about to prepare. "I will do all I can to keep healthy," she said. "I want a strong body when I serve God in Africa. After all, the Bible says God has chosen my body to be His home. I want to be careful how I treat it."

Dorothy enrolled in classes that would later prove useful. She and other students started Sunday schools in out-of-the-way places in the Breathitt County mountains. Together they devised a system they called "watching and praying."

"When I pray," suggested Dorothy, "you watch the kids and make them behave. When you pray, I'll watch."

She finished her studies at KMBI and went on to college in Iowa. There, one day, she received a surprise—the letter from George Thomas.

George and Dorothy on their wedding day.

Chapter 3

HERE COMES THE BRIDE

George and Dorothy's friendship grew as they exchanged letters. After a few months, she invited George to visit her at the Hughes's home in Kentucky. There, they saw each other for the first time. They fell in love before long and began to plan their wedding.

George visited his parents in Oregon later that summer. He and his father drove one day to the Friends conference grounds at Twin Rocks, close to the Pacific Ocean. As soon as they arrived, George saw Joseph Reece, a man he had known before.

"George," said Mr. Reece, "Edna and Rachel Chilson just left. They told us they're needing missionaries in Africa. You should contact them."

This news excited George. "With all their years of experience in Africa, I'm sure they can help me," he said. He found out the Chilsons' address in Wichita, Kansas, and wrote to them. They replied, *Stop and see us on your way back to Kentucky.*

When he got to Wichita, he stopped at Friends University to find out where to go. He told the registrar his reason for being there. She replied, "My sister, Rachel Chance, is on the mission board for Kansas Yearly Meeting of Friends. She'll want to meet you."

George talked with Mrs. Chance a few hours later. "I'm going to call the members of the Missionary Candidate Committee together," she said.

Before long, George met with the committee. "We would like you to stay for our annual Mission Board meeting that begins in a few days," one member said.

Another asked, "George, do you plan to get married?"

"Yes. I'm marrying a young woman from Kentucky. She's attending school in Iowa right now." Before George knew it, someone had arranged for Dorothy to come to Wichita for the upcoming meeting.

It did not take long for the Mission Board to decide they wanted George and Dorothy as their missionaries in Burundi (Burr-OOHN-dee), Africa.

"It would be easier to get your passports and to make other arrangements if you could be married right away," suggested the chairman.

"Now while you're here, we mean," someone else explained.

"Tonight during the annual missionary rally would be a good time for your wedding."

And so began that busy day—October 15, 1943. George and Dorothy dashed off to buy the marriage license and a wedding ring. Next, Rachel Chilson took Dorothy to a downtown department store to purchase a bride's dress. Other friends offered to furnish flowers and prepare the wedding reception.

That evening, the organist played the familiar wedding march at the beginning of the rally. People in the congregation looked startled. "What's going on?" they asked each other.

Edna Chilson stepped to the front of the platform a few moments later. George Thomas, wearing his gray suit, took his place beside the altar rail. Then, everyone saw Dorothy slowly walking down the aisle in her shiny white satin gown.

"It's a wedding!" they exclaimed.

Mrs. Chilson performed the short ceremony. After their friends greeted them at the reception, George and Dorothy spent a few days together. Dorothy traveled back to Iowa the next week to finish college. George collected his belongings in Kentucky and moved to Wichita to work for a building contractor.

Just before Christmas Dorothy completed her studies. She set off for Wichita to join George in their final preparations for going to Burundi. George wrote to his draft board in Oregon to let them know he had been appointed as a missionary to Africa. He also requested permission to leave the country.

The clerk replied by letter. *You may feel free to leave the United States. We believe this type of soldier is as helpful to the security of our country as the other kind.*

George and Dorothy started their three-month journey to Burundi on April 23, 1944. With the Second World War still going on, they chose to travel on a Portuguese ship. "It will be safer for us because Portugal is a neutral country," George explained.

High above the deck waved the large flag with PORTUGAL printed in huge letters all could see for at least a mile. Day and night the *Serpa Pinto's* lights blazed as it forged across the Atlantic Ocean. The ship's captain skillfully steered in a zigzag course to avoid German submarines.

Other missionaries had also chosen to travel on the *Serpa Pinto*. "God is protecting us," they all assured one another.

George and Dorothy stayed in Lisbon, Portugal, for two weeks. Next, they boarded another ship headed for Luanda, Angola, on the west coast of Africa. They traveled from there by truck, train, river boat, public bus, and lake steamer. At last they saw Burundi.

Trees of many kinds outlined the hills and mountains with several shades of green. Bright blossoms added special touches of color. Bujumbura, the capital city, bustled with people riding bicycles or going about on foot. Other residents pushed their way onto crowded public buses. Some riders carried squawking chickens or lugged

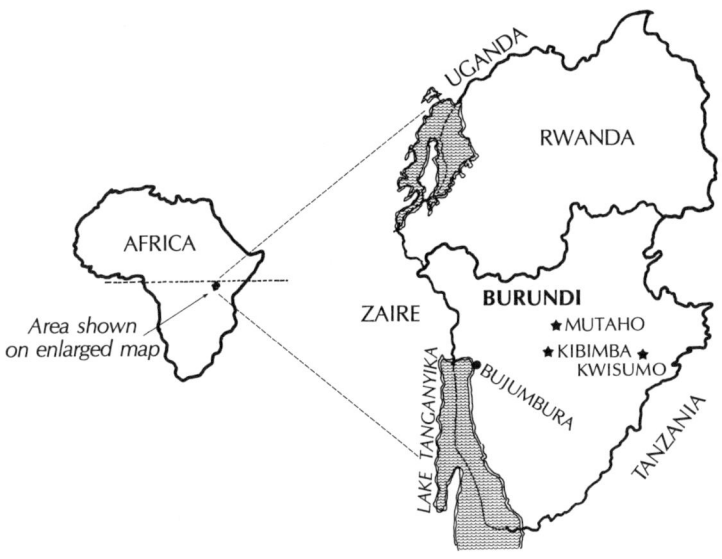

heavy bundles of vegetables. Raggedy beggars huddled on street corners. With outstretched hands, they cried pitifully, "Have mercy! Have mercy!"

A few rough, one-track roads twisted this way and that out from Bujumbura. In the dry season, bare feet pounded country paths into dirt-cement. The paths turned into rivers of squishy mud during the yearly wet season.

Most of the people called Barundi (Bah-ROON-dee) lived in small villages located among the mountains. Many of them spent their entire lifetimes within their own communities. Each family *urugo* (oo-ROO-go), a cluster of round, thatch-roofed huts, had protective fences of poles or thorn bushes. A ring of banana trees outside the enclosure provided almost complete privacy.

George and Dorothy soon discovered the friendliness of the Barundi. Their white-toothed smiles looked like sunshine in their black faces. Shiny-headed adults and kinky-haired children welcomed these newcomers to the Mutaho (Moo-TAH-hoe) mission station.

Ten years before, Ralph and Esther Choate had gone to live at Mutaho. The Barundi had acted afraid of these white missionaries at first.* Gradually, however, their fear had gone. Now, the villagers regularly worshiped on Sundays in the chapel built of interlaced sticks and mud. They freely attended classes there during the week, too.

The Thomases moved into the simple clay-brick house. They prepared to teach and preach, as well as to learn the Kirundi (Key-ROON-dee) language. As they settled into their new life at Mutaho, George and Dorothy had no idea of all that yet would come.

For more about Burundi and the Choates, read What Will Tomorrow Bring? *by Betty M. Hockett.*

Chapter 4

THE FIERY ACCIDENT

Rosemary Joy [*first Baby* handwritten] Thomas arrived on December 29, 1946, delighting her parents. "I have never seen a father as proud as George," said the nurse.

Besides taking care of Rosemary, Dorothy taught classes at the Mutaho grade school. She sometimes helped the missionary doctor at the clinic, also. "I'm not a nurse," she said, "but I can take temperatures and help clean out sores."

George had charge of the Mutaho mission station, supervising the school and the church. He regularly checked the outschools in out-of-the-way places among the hills, as well. He also drove to the Kibimba (Key-BEAM-ba) mission station to make sure everything ran smoothly there.*

On weekends, George and Dorothy packed their camping gear and traveled out among the hill churches. They drove their pickup until the road petered out, then hiked the rest of the way.

For more about Kibimba and Geraldine Custer, nurse, read Keeping Them All in Stitches, *by Betty M. Hockett.*

Barundi men, who traveled with them, helped carry the tent, bedding, food, pans, dishes, clothes, and drinking water. At each location, the Thomases preached as well as encouraged the Christians.

Dorothy took a good look at the path that led to one mountain location and said, "That's too straight up for me." She quickly found two sticks to use as supports during the steep climb.

The African men striding along behind laughed. "Now you have four legs," they said.

George made a special wooden chair for Rosemary to use on another trip to an outstation. "Two of the men can carry her in this chair," he suggested. They had no more than started up the hill when it began to rain. The path quickly turned to slippery goo. The carriers slid, stumbled, and then dropped Rosemary into the mud. She howled at the top of her voice, refusing to climb back into the chair.

That evening, George and the men set up the tent inside the school building. The roof leaked, but the tent kept the missionaries dry.

Arriving back at Mutaho late at night, the Thomases usually found the two watchmen asleep on the job. "They're not much help," said George.

"What if a wild animal or a thief comes when they're asleep?" Dorothy wanted to know.

A smile slowly spread across George's face as he said, "I'll teach the watchmen a lesson."

The next time the Thomases got home, the sleeping watchmen lay sprawled out. George quietly moved the spears the men had stuck into the ground nearby. Then he let out a loud howl that sounded exactly like a wild animal.

The watchmen bounded up and grabbed for their spears. Not finding them, they darted around, bumping into each other. Seconds later they discovered George standing out of sight in the shadows. Then they knew it had all been a trick.

George and Dorothy sometimes traveled east of Mutaho to the Kwisumo (Kwee-SOO-moe) area.

"I want to start a mission station here," said George. He pointed to the thatch-roofed huts located all around. "These people have no church close by."

His idea grew. Alfred Miller, another Friends missionary, often went with George to Kwisumo. Each time they camped there they worked on their plans for the new mission station.

"There's a shortage of building poles here," George pointed out to Alfred. "We don't want to waste the poles, so we'll use stone for the chapel as well as for the missionaries' house."

Little by little they built the chapel that would also provide space for school classes. They constructed a two-room house of stone and laid on the thatched roof. Then George, Dorothy, and Rosemary moved from Mutaho to live in their little stone house.

Dorothy spent lots of time keeping their home in order. They did not have electricity or hot, running water. Kerosene lanterns provided light. The wood-burning cook stove heated water for baths, dishes, and laundry.

Every day Dorothy boiled big pots of water for safe drinking. She cleaned the fruits and vegetables carefully to get rid of bugs and germs. Since she had no prepared mixes, she made everything herself. She and Rosemary churned butter to eat on their fresh-from-the-oven bread. "We ate well," said Rosemary a long time after their Burundi days.

Dorothy set up her small sewing machine and made colorful curtains for their windows. With one hand she turned the wheel. She guided the cloth under the needle with the other hand. It took a long time to sew one seam.

Some of the young African women learned from Dorothy how to sew for themselves. They chatted and giggled while stitching dresses and warm quilts from the pretty cloth Kansas women had sent.

As her days filled with more and more work, Dorothy said, "I need help here at home."

Soon, she hired an African man. Dorothy taught him to heat the flatirons on the stove before ironing the clothes he scrubbed by hand. He learned to cook meat and vegetables the way the Americans preferred them. After a while he could bake bread that Dorothy described as *wonderful*.

George spent many daylight hours building outschools. He often climbed onto the topmost ridgepole to nail the rafters together. Straddling the skinny pole, he looked out across the valley and hillsides. Sometimes he saw women carrying large containers of river water on their heads. Men hurried along the paths. Boys and girls scampered about, hilarious in their play. Others helped their mothers in the gardens.

This simple building will be like a lighthouse in this area, George thought. *These people need to hear about Jesus, the Light of the world. I hope a good, loving congregation will develop in this place.* George prayed for the people at work or play far below.

The Barundi soon discovered that buildings George had anything to do with looked good and held up well. "I'm glad Dad taught me how to be a good carpenter," he said.

At night George and Dorothy studied and read beside the kerosene lamp. George prepared Bible lessons and messages for the Sunday services at Kwisumo. Dorothy made charts for her reading classes.

People often came to the Thomas house. "Please help us know how to obey God," many of them said. George and Dorothy always had time to talk and pray with them.

Everyone around soon learned of George's love for hunting. They also recognized his shooting skills. He grew accustomed to taking his gun along on trips. There might come an unplanned opportunity to hunt for a new supply of meat for his family. Or, he might suddenly face unexpected danger.

"Oh, oh! There's a python," said George to Clayton Brown, also a Friends missionary, as they headed upcountry one day. "We mustn't let it get away." The python's pretty camouflage-patterned skin did not deceive them.

"If we don't kill it, it's apt to eat goats in the nearby villages," Clayton whispered.

"Or worse yet, go after people."

Several feet of the python abruptly disappeared into a wild pig's burrow. The rest of it lay out in plain sight. "I'm going to pull the snake out," said George. "Get ready to shoot as soon as you see its head."

George grasped the tail, which felt as big around as a baseball bat. He pulled and pulled and pulled, stepping backward as more of the snake gradually appeared.

Out came the head. Clayton pulled the trigger. The python went limp. Together the two men skinned it.

In 1949, George, Dorothy, and Rosemary returned for a visit to the United States. Sometimes George told his python story. People usually gasped as he casually unrolled the thirteen-foot snake skin.

That year in the United States still stands out as a difficult one. First, Dorothy's father died in July. Dorothy felt sad, but she thanked God all over again for her happy childhood. The Thomases then moved to Newberg, Oregon. George signed up once more for classes at Pacific College, newly named George Fox College.

In November, George and Dorothy welcomed the birth of Elizabeth Ann. They held their beautiful baby and made plans for her care. God, though, had His own special plans for Elizabeth.

Quite unexpectedly, she went to heaven to be with Him.

George and Dorothy could hardly believe what had happened. With God's help, however, they spent the next few months recovering from this shock.

The Thomas family left the United States at the end of the summer in 1950. The next five months in Belgium gave them the opportunity to learn French, the business language of Burundi. At the end of that time, they headed back to their home at Kwisumo.

They quickly organized their daily routines. George heard about several places needing new buildings. He also preached and traveled around to oversee other parts of the mission work.

Besides working with the Kwisumo women, Dorothy taught Rosemary her school lessons. The family had devotions and prayer at breakfast. In the evening, they read Bible stories and prayed again. They also read many books together.

George and Dorothy permitted a succession of exotic pets. Chameleons, monkeys, lizards, and small antelopes called duikers all added to the family fun.

One day George suggested to his father, also a missionary in Burundi at that time, "While Dorothy gets dinner, let's go out and do a little target practice."

With their guns in hand, they walked behind the house. "You shoot first," George offered. Clyde Thomas shot. He missed the target. George shot next, and that bullet also whizzed past the mark.

Just then, Dorothy stepped out to announce dinner. "Looks like neither of you can hit the broadside of an elephant. I could do better," she said, laughing.

George handed his rifle to Dorothy without saying anything. She lifted the gun to her right shoulder, squinted, aimed, and shot. POW! The bullet sailed straight to the center of the target. She gave the gun back to George, saying quietly, "Dinner's ready."

Sometimes George and Dorothy drove the narrow, bouncy roads to the other mission stations or to Bujumbura. One day, Lawrence and Delores Ehinger, Friends missionaries, rode back to Kwisumo with them.

"Look at that beautiful leopard," exclaimed Lawrence.

The sleek, graceful animal leaped off the road and disappeared among the trees. A few miles farther on, George's car lurched as the motor gasped. Then it stopped. George tried over and over to start the car again. Each time, the motor only made a strange grinding noise.

Finally George said, "We're just at the top edge of a valley. This road goes down the hill and up the other side. Lawrence, would you and the women mind getting out to push? Maybe I can start the car as I coast down the hill."

Dorothy peered anxiously out the window. "I hope that leopard doesn't have his mate around here somewhere," she said.

"Try not to think about it," encouraged George.

The three passengers climbed out. They glanced about nervously as they pushed the car. It gradually gained speed while coasting down the hill. Suddenly, the motor coughed back to life. Dorothy and the Ehingers hurried to catch up.

"Boy, I hope that leopard isn't nearby," muttered Dorothy. She ran as fast as when she had won first prize in the children's race at the school fair. When the three runners reached the car, they threw themselves inside and slammed the doors.

"Am I ever glad that leopard didn't come back," said Dorothy, her heart still pounding.

Trouble also developed with the car another time. Stopping at Mutaho for the night, George discovered the problem. "I've already soldered this gas tank twice and now it's leaking again. I'll see if I can fix it while we're here."

He drove the car into the three-sided garage that had a pit underneath. Carefully, he drained the gas into a big can and deposited it safely outside. George rummaged around in the garage until he found the blowtorch and solder. With his hands full, he climbed down into the pit where he had a good view of the leaky tank. The crack showed plainly. George turned on the blowtorch and reached up.

POOF! Instantly, the blowtorch ignited gas fumes. A violent fire erupted in the pit. Flames caught George's shirt. The cloth shriveled and baked onto his skin. His hair, eyebrows, and eyelashes also caught on fire.

He threw down the blowtorch and struggled up the ladder. Moments later, George stumbled through the door of the mission house.

Chapter 5

PEOPLE-EATING LIONS

Rosemary screamed at the sight of her scorched father. Skin hung off his arms in tatters. His singed hair stuck up like black stubble.

The missionaries, who had been enjoying tea together, gasped. "Quick! Wrap him in wet towels!" someone urged.

Louisa Ammerman, a missionary with World Gospel Mission, helped Dorothy carefully snip away George's melted shirt.

"I'll be right back with my car and take him to the hospital," said another Friends missionary, James Morris. By the time he returned, the women had George bundled up in cold, sopping towels.

The dusty trip to the hospital at Ibuye (Ee-BOO-yea), north of Mutaho, took more than an hour. Upon arriving, the missionaries found that the two doctors had gone elsewhere. A nurse on duty looked at George and said confidently, "I know how to care for burns. I lived through the blitz in London during the war."

She examined him, then said, "You have burns over sixty percent of your body. You'll need skin grafts." She wrapped him in so many bandages he looked like a big snowman. His burned face swelled until only little eye-holes showed in the mound of puffy flesh.

Meanwhile, word about George's fiery accident arrived at the Kibimba mission station. "He could die at any time," the missionaries said.

"I hear he needs plasma," one of them reminded the others.

They gathered for prayer that evening and afterward discussed the situation. "Should I go to Bujumbura to get the plasma George needs?" asked Lawrence Ehinger.

"Perhaps you ought to stay here and build a coffin for him in case he dies," someone else suggested.

In the end, they decided Lawrence would go to Bujumbura.

He had trouble finding the owner of the drugstore that Sunday morning. Finally, he located him, and together they hurried to the storage warehouse.

"The plasma's in here," the man said. His fingers fumbled for the key, first in his left shirt pocket, then his right. He felt both pants pockets. No key.

Lawrence stood by, feeling more anxious by the minute.

"I'll have to break in," the man said. He seized a big rock and smashed the lock. Lawrence quickly paid for the plasma and rushed back to the hospital.

"How do I look?" George asked. Lawrence remembered the week before when malaria medicine had made George's skin look yellow. "Well," he replied, "at least you don't look yellow now."

News of George's serious accident and his need for skin grafts quickly spread to missionaries and others in several countries. An African man wrote to his good friend, George, and generously offered, *You may have some of my skin.*

Many people prayed, however, and George's body miraculously healed with no need for skin grafts.

For a long time after that, his arms and hands had a polka-dot look. Sometimes people asked about the white spots. George laughingly explained, "Well, you know I work close to the leper colony."

The person asking appeared shocked at the idea that George had leprosy. After that, he always said truthfully, "These white scars are the places where the shirt burned onto my skin."

Eventually, the polka dots healed and George's hands and arms again looked normal.

* * *

George, Dorothy, and Rosemary traveled to the United States in 1956. A few months later, they announced the birth of Rebecca Jane, soon nicknamed Becky.

They all returned to Burundi where Becky grew from babyhood into a busy toddler. They easily settled into village life once again. "We're glad you are back," their Barundi friends told them.

Every Sunday morning, the four of them walked to Sunday school. Once, 63 children jammed into the little chapel. *Most of their parents don't know Jesus as their Savior*, Dorothy thought. *But how thankful I am that these boys and girls have heard about Him.*

If enough small Bible story pictures had come in packages from the United States, Dorothy handed them out to the children each Sunday. The boys and girls waited impatiently, not caring whether the pictures fit that day's story or not.

One day she visited the hut of a little girl who attended Sunday school. A row of Bible story pictures hung unevenly along one grass-reed wall. "They were the only pictures in their home," Dorothy told George later.

"We'll pray they will be a reminder that Jesus wants to be their Savior," he replied.

On a certain Sunday, one little girl arrived at church completely naked.

Afterward, Rosemary burst into tears. "She doesn't have any clothes."

Dorothy put an arm around Rosemary. "I'm sure her family is too poor to buy a dress. Let's make one for her."

The next morning, she and Rosemary cut out a girl-sized dress from a big, clean cloth sack. They pinned the pieces together, and Dorothy sewed the seams. Rosemary selected bright red trimming.

"That's a prettier dress than anyone else has," she said.

"We had better charge a tiny bit for the dress," Dorothy suggested. "Otherwise everyone will want one, and we'll have more to do than we can manage."

When Dorothy gave the dress to the girl, she said, "Tell your mother she can bring us five eggs sometime to pay for this new dress."

The girl came two Sundays later as bare as before. "Where's her dress?" Rosemary whispered to Dorothy.

"I don't know for sure," Dorothy replied quietly.

Even as they wondered, the older sister arrived with the new dress in hand. She proceeded to put it on the younger girl. Dorothy leaned over and told Rosemary, "Her mother may have thought the dress would get dirty or torn if she wore it on the way to church."

Two months later, the mother brought the five eggs to Dorothy as payment for the dress.

* * *

Antelope, wild pigs, and monkeys regularly helped themselves to sweet potatoes and beans from hillside or valley gardens. One season, villagers complained to George, "A hippopotamus comes every night and eats our gardens. We're afraid we won't have anything left to harvest."

"A hippo can eat a lot of garden in one night," George agreed.

Early the next morning he and Lawrence Ehinger set out with their guns to find the thieving hippo. "I'm sure he'll be in the river close to those gardens," George said.

As they got near the water, they stopped and waited. Sure enough, the monstrous dark gray hippo-head emerged from the water.

"One, two, three, shoot!" George yelled. Both men shot and hit the hippopotamus. Straightaway it sank out of sight.

The men waited for it to surface again. Nothing happened. After an hour, George fastened one end of a long rope around his waist. "Tie the other end to a tree," he told Lawrence. "I'm going to wade out and see if I can feel the hippo with my feet. Keep your rifle handy in case you need to shoot again."

George splashed into the water while Lawrence stood with his gun ready for action. All remained quiet in the river. Two more steps, and George turned back to shore.

"You aren't afraid of anything," Lawrence said. "What if that hippo had still been alive?"

The men eventually heard that the dead hippopotamus had floated downstream. Africans hauled it out of the water, butchered it, and sold the meat at market.

Villagers also had other animal troubles. Leopards ate their goats. Lions, which wandered north from Tanzania, also fed upon Burundi goats, calves, and other livestock. Sometimes, they attacked and ate people, too.

Great fear settled over the area the time three people-eating lions began to roam and kill. "Once lions become people-eaters, they tend to continue," said George. No one felt safe.

The casualties increased. Four people one night, an entire family of ten soon after, on and on. The tribal chief from across the river pleaded with George, "Please come kill these lions. They have eaten more than 100 people already." George accepted the challenge, inviting Lawrence Ehinger to hunt with him sometimes.

"I have an idea where those lions may run through tonight," George said to Lawrence one morning. "Let's build a platform up in a tree where we can wait for them. We'll put a cow in a pen underneath to attract the lions."

The men nailed several strong boards together, then secured the platform well above the ground. Before dark, they penned up the cow, climbed the tree, and settled down to watch.

No lions showed up.

On another day, the two missionary men decided the lions would circle through a certain valley that night. They drove into the valley at evening, just as it began to rain.

Right away the road turned to slick-as-grease mud. The pickup wheels spun helplessly. Soon they had mired too deeply to go any farther. "We'll have to spend the night in our pickup," said George. They sat inside all night, swatting at mosquitoes, praying, and telling stories. Finally, daylight came. The men got out to unkink their legs.

"Look here, Lawrence," said George, pointing to the ground. "Leopard tracks. While we waited for the lions, a leopard evidently looked us over."

"Those tracks go all the way around the pickup," Lawrence observed. "He really had a good look at us."

The men found out later the lions they had hoped to see had prowled near that valley, killing one woman.

Soon, the lions began killing people in an area where missionaries sometimes had camped and hunted. The local chief sent a letter to George, *Please come help us hunt these lions.*

That time, George called on Knud Dahl, a Danish missionary working at the leper colony near Kwisumo, to help him. "There used to be a Barundi family here who brought milk to us whenever we camped," George explained when they arrived at the site. "The lions ate the whole family."

The chief and some of his men joined in the hunt, along with George and Knud. While they all discussed what to do first, they heard the lions roar. "Now we know where they are," George said, immediately bristling with energy. "Lions have big feet. They're easy to follow."

He led the way into the thick brush. The men quickly found fresh tracks. "See that open space up ahead?" George whispered. "If we can force the lions out there, we can get a good shot." He instructed the chief and his men to move about while making lots of racket. They all knew lions usually ran away from a loud commotion.

The plan worked. A big lioness hurried into the open space. George and Knud shot, and she dropped dead. The other two lions ran off into the brush.

A few weeks later, George came upon a group of distressed people. "What happened?" he wanted to know.

"A lion killed an old woman who lived on the hill just above the chief's house," a young man explained in an irate voice.

After a brief discussion with the Africans, George hurried off to get Knud. They gathered together a group of willing hunters, including the chief.

George crept toward the brush where the lions might hide that time of day. Sure enough, he saw the movement of golden fur. George and Knud held a quick, whispered consultation before dashing off to circle around in front of the lions. A few minutes later they scrambled onto a knoll, intending to see the lions again as they passed beside the river. The African chief arrived a few steps behind them. He stopped at the base of the knoll, also looking toward the river.

Suddenly, a terrifying roar filled the air.

Chapter 6

A CHANGE OF SCENERY

The chief darted sideways as the lion sprang toward him. All three men fired. They shot the lion dead. The other lion jumped into the river and swam away.

The hunters gathered around the body of killer-lion number two. No one cared to even think about what would have happened if the chief had not moved or if the shots had missed.

A few weeks later, killer-lion number three crashed into a grass-roofed hut and killed eight people. George, Knud, and several Barundi hunters stalked the lion the next day. Before nighttime, George and Knud shot and killed it, much to the relief of all.

* * *

The next time they arrived in the United States, George and Dorothy explained, "We'll stay longer than usual. Rosemary needs to have braces put on her teeth."

They moved to South Texas, where George found a job in a factory.

"Dorothy, God spoke to me at work today," he said one evening. "I believe He wants us to be missionaries to the Navajo (NAH-vuh-hoe) Indians. What do you think?"

Dorothy smiled. "I've already been thinking about it." She went on to describe a book she had read a few days before. "It reminded me how some people in our country treated the Indians so badly. We really owe them a lot."

"I wonder if we have missionaries on the Navajo reservation?" George asked.

A phone call from Colorado brought the answer before that weekend. "Our Friends mission to the Navajo Indians needs more missionaries," said the church leader at the other end of the line. "I recently talked to members of your mission board. They gave permission for you and Dorothy to work with the Navajos at Rough Rock, Arizona, for the next two years."

It did not take long for George and Dorothy to say "Yes," to this new plan. They would have no time out from missionary work, after all.

"To move from the heart of Africa to the center of the Navajo reservation is quite a change of scenery," they said.

The unique rock formations of Arizona amazed George and Dorothy. They marveled at the slender rock spires rising toward the blue sky often speckled with marshmallowy clouds. The sandy desert continually looked as if an artist had been busy with a paint brush.

Vern and Lois Ellis, who had already worked at Rough Rock for several years, helped the Thomases get acquainted.* George and Dorothy learned to love Navajo people of all ages. They met Aszan, a thin, wrinkled old lady who lived up on Black Mountain. She could barely see, although she had good hearing and a keen memory.

"Members of her family have been unfriendly to our work," Vern explained. "Even so, we had a service in her home last winter. Aszan told us afterward she liked the gospel story, but she didn't feel ready to accept it."

George and Dorothy helped with camp meeting and assisted in the first Bible training program for Navajo adults. They also visited many Indian homes situated in groups called *camps*.

Getting to these clusters of hogans or cabins meant a hazardous drive on narrow, rutty roads up Black Mountain. When it rained, the roads reminded George of the slick mud in Burundi. The dust, which coated everything during dry times, also made him think of Africa.

One day, George and Willie Draper, a Navajo worker, drove up the mountain to visit a camp. One of Aszan's sons saw them.

"My mother is sick," he said. "We want you to come see her."

*Read more about Rough Rock, the Navajo reservation, and Vern and Lois Ellis in Mud on Their Wheels, by Betty M. Hockett.

George and Willie agreed to stop at Aszan's camp on their way back to Rough Rock. When they got there, Willie said, "See that new hogan away from the family camp? That's Aszan's death-hogan. Most Navajos believe they can't use a hogan if someone dies in it. Aszan's family put her in the new one so they won't have to abandon her good home after she dies."

George and Willie entered the small, round death-hogan. Aszan looked more thin and wrinkled than ever. "We should take you to the hospital," George said.

"No," replied Aszan faintly. "I would die on the way."

The two men talked about what they should do. "I'll give her some medicine," said George. He opened his kit and carefully measured out the proper dose. As he gave it to Aszan, George whispered to Willie, "This may also be our last chance to help her accept Jesus."

Willie nodded and knelt down beside Aszan. "You have tried everything except Jesus."

"Yes," the old lady agreed.

"Jesus can help you. He's the only One who can save you."

The Navajo woman raised up on her elbows. "I want Jesus to save me. I want to go to heaven."

George and Willie then prayed with Aszan. On their way down the mountain later, George said, "We may not see her on earth again, but it's good to know she'll be in heaven."

Aszan's neighbors reported surprising news two weeks later. "Her family says she was dying but the missionaries prayed for her and gave her some medicine. Now she says she feels strong enough to go to the hospital."

After a few days there, Aszan improved so much the doctors said she could go home. George took her back up the mountain. "I was sinking down, but the Lord raised me up," Aszan said. "I'm going to hold on to Him as long as I live."

As Aszan gained strength, her family became friendlier toward the missionaries.

* * *

With Rosemary's dental work complete, George and Dorothy knew the time had come to return to Burundi. That meant making a difficult decision: Rosemary would stay behind to finish high school and go on to college.

"We'll be glad to have her live with us," Uncle David and Aunt Florence Thomas said.

George, Dorothy, and Becky could hardly bear to say goodbye to Rosemary. They somehow did, however, and she settled into her new home overlooking Netarts Bay in Tillamook County, Oregon. Later, she would visit them in Burundi. The others would travel to the United States for her wedding to Michael Livingston in 1965. In the meantime, God would help them endure the separation.

Once they arrived back in Burundi, George soon had plenty of building projects lined up.

Dorothy taught women's classes and also organized Becky's school work each day.

As before, they liked to drive throughout the beautiful mountains, encouraging the Barundi pastors and their families. Many times, an old African man named Ndabashinze (Dob-a-SHEEN-zee) went with them.

One Sunday, they all visited the worship service at the leper colony, where Ndabashinze had organized a group of believers. The service included a welcome to new members. The old African marched in with his head held high. Those with leprosy followed. Some hobbled slowly and painfully because the disease had crippled their feet. Several had fingers missing. Their hands appeared almost useless. Even so, smiles brightened all of the disfigured faces.

They look like the happiest people in the world, Dorothy thought.

"I'm glad I have leprosy," testified one man. "If I had not been here, I would not have heard about Jesus."

Now and then, George and Dorothy took a few days of holiday in Rwanda (GWAN-duh), a country next to Burundi.

They never thought that someday they would live there. Certainly they had no notion they would have any part in a miracle that would happen in Rwanda.

As they traveled from place to place, Dorothy always supported George with her love and humor.

Sometimes, though, she appeared somewhat nervous as cows and people wandered carelessly onto the road. "I'll take care of that problem," George told her one day. The next week he installed a horn on Dorothy's side of the car. "Now you can sound a warning."

Dorothy had a special ability to make Africans feel welcome in their home. She always served coffee or tea with lots and lots of sugar, as well as bread for dunking.

No matter who knocked at their door day or night, Dorothy welcomed them. Almost as soon as she said "Hello," she would disappear into her kitchen. A few moments later, she handed plates of delicious food to her guests.

"Dorothy always served the best she had," friends said later, "even if all she could rustle up at the time would be bread and eggs." They also remember her endless array of cookies.

Missionary children never forgot the little poems and songs Aunt Dot pulled out for every occasion. Uncle George also had a wonderful fund of stories and sayings the children still recalled years later.

Dorothy got up early to read her Bible and pray. Writing letters at the dining table took up some of her early morning time. People who received the letters said, "She's a wonderful letter writer. She keeps us informed."

Every day, a beggar woman named Hannah limped along the dirt path to sit beside the

Thomases' back door. Ugly sores covered her hands and feet. Everyone in the village knew she lived in filth, and that she wore clothes the church gave to her.

"She has such a sad face," said Becky. "See how her lower lip hangs down?"

"Here, Becky," said Dorothy. "You carry the bread and I'll take this bowl of soup to Hannah." They offered food to the beggar every day. Dorothy often rubbed ointment on the sores.

Other people, also, regularly appeared at Dorothy's back door for first aid. She cleaned wounds, sprinkled sulfa powder on them to prevent infections, and taped bandages. Many people welcomed her medicine for their sore eyes.

In 1972, George and Dorothy left Burundi. They moved to Newberg, Oregon, expecting to return to Africa soon.

Time passed for George and Dorothy as Becky finished high school. During that time, war had broken out between two tribes in Burundi. The Thomases began to ask themselves, "Shall we go back to Burundi or not?" They could not decide.

In the middle of their dilemma, they heard from a friend in Klamath Falls, Oregon. He suggested something they had not thought about before.

Chapter 7

THE BEGINNING OF A MIRACLE

"Would you consider going to Sprague River as the pastor?" their friend asked on the phone that day.

"We'll pray about it," George and Dorothy replied. Neither felt excited about moving to that tiny southern Oregon community.

A month later, George and Dorothy stood at the kitchen sink peeling apples. "All I can think of is Sprague River," he said.

"If you feel that strongly about it, you had better say we'll go," Dorothy replied.

This new challenge quickly erased thoughts of returning to Burundi. A few days later they headed south. Once again, the Thomases had no time out.

"I'm glad we'll be among Klamath and Modoc Indians," Dorothy told George on their way to Sprague River. "I still feel we owe a debt to our American Indians. Our forefathers didn't treat them fairly."

"They need our Savior, too," George added.

The Friends Church congregation of twenty, which included only one native American, turned out to be even smaller than George and Dorothy had thought. "We're the only church in town," George remarked. "We must find ways to get acquainted with people who never attend."

Dorothy joined the Home Extension group. George attended the Lions Club. He also served as a volunteer firefighter. They both signed up for classes on emergency medical procedures. They passed the course, and afterward George regularly took his turn on the ambulance crew.

One night he rode with the ambulance out into the country. "We're after a man who cut his leg with a chain saw," the driver explained.

When George saw the injury, he thought, *A saw didn't make this cut. A saw cuts ragged. This is a clean-edged knife wound.*

The crew stopped the bleeding, then headed the ambulance toward the hospital. George helped unload their patient at the emergency entrance.

Suddenly, the man protested hoarsely. "No! No! Don't take me in there. See those guys? One of 'em knifed me. They're waitin' to get me again." George helped reload him into the ambulance. They stayed out of sight until after the police took the other men away.

Later, George told Dorothy, "The whole story finally came out. You see, there had been a big fight. Our patient had stabbed one of those three men he saw waiting inside. The others brought that guy in to get sewed up, then hung around to wait for the man we had. They knew he would show up at the hospital sooner or later. They all would have gone at it again if they had had a chance."

The Thomases loved the people of Sprague River. Many came to the pastor and his wife, where they always found comfort for sad or troublesome situations. George also performed weddings and preached at funerals.

Gradually, both whites and Indians began to fill the tiny church each Sunday. "We need more space," George said, thinking about how to build new rooms onto the church.

"Neither of us would have chosen this job, but we have learned a lot," said Dorothy. "God makes up for what we don't know how to do."

After seven years, the congregation had grown to seventy regular attenders. The parsonage and church looked good with the new rooms as well as other changes. George and Dorothy knew the time had come for them to leave. "It's not easy to go," they said.

The Sprague River congregation always fondly remembered George and Dorothy. Some years later, they named one section of their church building "Thomas Hall."

George and Dorothy moved back to their blue house at the edge of the George Fox College campus in Newberg. George remarked one day,

"It's been almost thirty years since we first went to Burundi."

They did not expect anyone to call upon them for further missionary service. Such a call did come, however, three years later.

We're starting missionary work in Rwanda, said the message from the Evangelical Friends Mission Board. *You have had lots of experience, and we want you to help.*

Rwanda! Happy memories flooded over George and Dorothy. Many of their Barundi friends now lived there. In fact, much of life in Rwanda resembled Burundi: hunting and driving licenses, money, and the French language. It all would make them feel right at home. Besides, Kinyarwanda (Keen-yuh-GWAN-duh), the tribal language, had only minor differences from Burundi's Kirundi.

Before long they said, "Yes, we will go to Rwanda." Willard Ferguson, a Friends missionary who had worked in Burundi, also agreed to go. "My family will join me when school is out," he added.

George and Dorothy hurried to get ready. They scheduled physical checkups, bought supplies, and packed. One day as Dorothy considered their work ahead, she felt anxious.

Dear Lord, she prayed, *I'm frightened at the thought of what is before me. I served You while I was young. You still are with me, though I am not as strong now. Please give me strength for each*

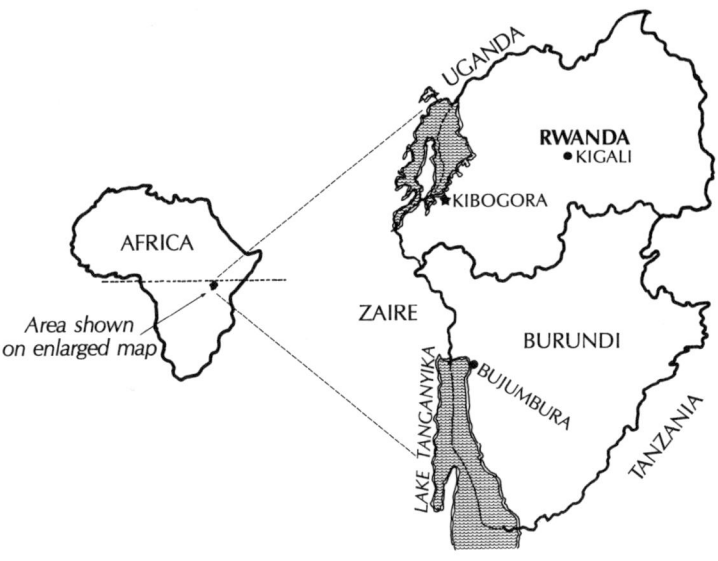

day. *I want to be like You, dear God. Go before us. Lead us to the place You have prepared.* As she read God's promises to go with her and help her, she felt comforted.

George said to their friends, "Ask God to lead us to the right people who can help us with our work."

Many people prayed, and the miracle in Rwanda got under way.

This small African country borders Burundi, Tanzania (Tan-za-KNEE-uh), Uganda (You-GHAN-duh), and Zaire (Zie-EAR). Its mild and sunny climate gives it the nickname, "Land of Eternal Spring." Steep mountains with rolling grasslands protect narrow, green valleys. Coffee and tea grow abundantly. The famous mountain gorillas live amidst the range of volcanoes in the northwest corner.

On February 21, 1986, the Thomases and Willard Ferguson arrived in Kigali (Key-GALL-ee), the capital city. They took extra time to pray the next day.

They also talked about all they had to do right away: buy a car, open a bank account, apply at the post office for a mailbox, and find a suitable house.

"We must get acquainted with the city," said George.

"Let's go for a walk and try to get our bearings," Dorothy suggested.

After a while they stood on a hill where they could see in several directions. Most of the people called Banyarwanda (Bahn-yuh-GWAN-duh) lived away from the bustling city. Their small, tin-roofed houses and tiny garden plots made a colorful patchwork spread out on the steep hillsides.

Barefooted men and women passed one another on the paths alongside the roads. Most of them balanced heavy bags of corn or big bunches of bananas on their heads.

"Let's find a garage that sells cars," George suggested. "Perhaps it would be down this way."

They passed three boys, busy with their play. "Look at their toy cars," Dorothy said in a low voice to George. "They've made them out of wire and string and sticks. And bits of plastic, too."

A common sight in Kigali.
Homemade fun for boys (below) in Kigali.

Five minutes later, the three Americans stopped to ask a stranger for directions.

"I should know you," he said.

"I taught for years in the Kibimba Normal School in Burundi," Willard replied.

The young man smiled. "Yes, that's where I knew you. I graduated from that school." He turned out to be the first of many Barundi friends they met in Rwanda.

The young man told the missionaries how to find the garage. There, George and Willard found a good car, but they did not buy it just then.

"Now to get on with what else we need to do," said George. In the next two hours, they discovered the difficulty of getting everything done.

They had to have extra pictures of themselves to secure a bank account. If they wanted a mailbox, they needed to write a letter to a post office official. Before doing that, however, they must talk to another official. They could not see him without transportation to get there.

After the merry-go-round of the morning's activities, George suggested, "Let's eat lunch." He led the way into a restaurant. All at once, he exclaimed, "Ed! Joan!" and almost tripped over his feet as he ran across the room.

The Rawsons, who had been missionaries in Burundi, looked at the newcomers in amazement. "George! Dorothy! Willard!" Everyone began to talk at once.

After the first excitement wore off, George said, "We knew you lived in Rwanda, and we had hoped to see you soon."

"Wasn't God good to bring us here where you would be eating lunch today?" Dorothy said as she hugged Joan once more.

Rawsons then told about their work in an agriculture project in northern Rwanda. "We come into the city fairly often," Ed said.

"You'll need transportation until you have your own car," Joan noted. "I'll be glad to come back and drive you around."

George quickly replied, "Thank you. We'll appreciate whatever you can do for us. I remember your help in Burundi meant a lot to us, too."

After lunch, the Thomases and Willard set out to do what they could that afternoon. Most of their efforts, however, turned to nothing.

"We're like the chicken and the egg," George said with a laugh. "You have to have a chicken to have an egg. On the other hand, you need an egg before you can get a chicken."

Dorothy laughed, too. "I see what you mean. We need an address before we can do much else. We can't get the address, though, until we do something."

"Aren't we glad God knows all about this?" remarked Willard.

A few days later, another missionary directed them to a house that turned out to be exactly what they had been looking for. Mr. Nathan, who owned the spacious home, said, "God answered my prayer. I asked Him to send renters who would live and work for the Lord."

"God answered our prayers, too," George added. "We asked Him for a comfortable place to live in an area that doesn't already have a lot of churches."

Dorothy shook hands with Mr. Nathan as she said, "We're happy to have a landlord who loves God."

At the end of the first week in Rwanda, George said, "I've certainly felt God's presence this week."

"Our job here won't be easy," said Willard. "The way God helped us this week, though, makes us know He'll help us with everything else."

Dorothy nodded, then added, "It's been wonderful to have Joan chauffeur us around." For years after, they all remembered how she helped them during their settling-in time.

"Now, our most important task is to get government recognition for our church," George said quietly.

Willard replied, "We can't organize a church here without it."

"We may face an impossible situation," said George. "After all, the government of Rwanda hasn't given recognition to any new churches for the last twenty years."

Many times in the next few months the Thomases and Fergusons would think for sure they faced an impossible situation.

Chapter 8

THE MERRY-GO-ROUND

Dorothy sewed, listening as George and Willard made plans.

"We must visit with Bishop Aaron of the Free Methodist Church," George said. "He was born and raised in Rwanda, so he'll know what we should do."

Willard agreed. "He knows our denomination since he graduated from our school at Kibimba. He also understands what we believe."

After several tries, they finally arranged an appointment with the bishop. "There are many opportunities to present the Gospel here," Bishop Aaron told the missionaries. "We cannot begin to keep up with the possibilities in Rwanda."

The Thomases and Willard felt encouraged. Their hope rose even higher when he added, "I'll be glad to help you in any way I can."

George spoke up quickly. "We're anxious to get government recognition for our church. How should we go about getting it?"

"If I were you," Bishop Aaron said, "I would go directly to the Minister of Justice."

"Can he give us the permission we need?" asked George.

"Yes," the bishop replied. "Let him know the most important job you will have is to lead people to accept Christ. Tell him that will help them live better lives."

The conversation ended with the bishop again assuring them he would do all he could to help. It sounded simpler than it actually turned out.

* * *

Soon after moving into their rented house, George and Willard visited Pastor Serukato of another church.

"You must have someone else ask the government to renew your visas," he told them. "Otherwise you cannot expect to get them. If you don't have visas, you'll have to leave the country."

"It all sounds like a merry-go-round," George replied. "We must have government recognition. Before we get that, however, we need to have land, a headquarters building, and church members. But we can't purchase land, build a building, or take in members until we have the government's okay to go ahead. To do all of that, we need a visa that allows us to stay."

Before the men left, Pastor Serukato prayed for them. Then he said, "Maybe you won't get permission from the government. There's a chance you

Patchwork fields outside of Kigali.

can't get your visas renewed, either. In the meantime, perhaps you will help one person accept Jesus as Savior. If so, you will have done something important. Later, you can come back and visit that person. By then he or she may have helped many others find the Savior, too."

George and Willard shook hands with the pastor. "I feel as if we have talked with a real man of God," said George.

* * *

Settling into their home took up some of the missionaries' time. Dorothy hand-sewed pretty curtains for all 16 windows. They bought furniture at a sale.

George spaded the garden plot, then planted flowers donated by new friends.

"Now we need someone to help with our housework," said Dorothy.

A young man knocked at their door two days later. "My name is Silas," he said. He handed a note to George.

"It's from Mr. Nathan, our landlord," he told Dorothy. "He says Silas is a good worker, and we may want to hire him to work for us."

The next day, George talked to others Silas had worked for, then hired him.

He swept the floors and dusted their furniture almost every day, and once a week he did the laundry. Before long, he learned how to shop for rice, beans, vegetables, and meat at the market. Silas cooked regular meals, including lots of potatoes, for the missionaries. Sometimes he baked huge cakes, too.

"Silas, this cake is more than we can eat," Dorothy would say. "Take some of it home to your family."

Silas also knew how to keep up the garden and yard. When the missionaries began to learn Kinyarwanda, he helped by listening to them practice the vocabulary and grammar.

"He's sure nice to have around," said George one evening.

"Another one of our prayers God answered," Dorothy noted.

* * *

"I want to invite your Friends Church to work under the registration of the Free Methodist Church," Bishop Aaron told George and Willard on March 11.

George looked pleased. "We had hoped something like this would work out."

"It's the best way to start fulfilling the government requirements for establishing your own church," the bishop explained.

The three men agreed to talk with others of their denominations. "We want final permission from all concerned," said George.

He and Willard rushed home to tell Dorothy the good news.

"Of course, a lot must happen before we can actually work with the Free Methodists," said George.

"I have an idea," said Dorothy as she hurried into the kitchen. She returned a few minutes later with glasses of fruit punch. "Let's celebrate what God has done for us."

After that, George and Willard had more talks with Bishop Aaron. They wanted to find out the best ways of working together. "We don't want to start in the wrong place or in the wrong way," said George. "We don't know where to organize a congregation," Willard explained. "We're anxious to begin as soon as we can, and where there's not much other church work."

They considered several locations around Kigali. "Lord, help us know what to do," George prayed. Soon, he sent an urgent request to Friends in the United States: *Pray for Rwanda.*

The missionaries began to plan for Easter. A Free Methodist pastor in Kigali had invited George to preach in his church on Easter Sunday. It would be George's first time to preach in the Kinyarwanda language. He carefully worked on his message, while Dorothy and Willard prayed for him.

The message turned out well. At least fifty people stayed to pray after George finished preaching. He said afterward, "I'm thankful I had the chance to preach. I praise the Lord for His blessing."

A few weeks later, the missionaries received a check in the mail. *This is the Easter offering from Evangelical Friends churches in the United States,* the letter stated. *Use it to buy a van for your work in Rwanda.*

This news delighted George and Willard. "We need another vehicle," they said.

Christians in the area heard about these new missionaries. Several groups came to the mission house. Most wanted to know if they could be part of the new church.

Dorothy welcomed all of their visitors and served tea and cookies to them. Sometimes guests unexpectedly stayed on through lunch. Dorothy wisely kept cooked beans frozen for quick thawing, heating, and serving. "I'm glad people here like juicy beans on rice," she told George one evening.

Two young men, Amos and Amminidab, came back again and again to talk to George. Amos already had experience as a preacher, although he earned his living as a chauffeur. Amminidab had preached, also. He had a good recommendation from a man George had known in Burundi. These two became special friends to George and Dorothy. They would later become the first workers in the new church.

Four months after arriving in Kigali, George and Dorothy received approval from the mission board to work with the Free Methodists. They also got their visas. "At last we've made some headway," Dorothy said.

The Thomases and the Fergusons made plans. George and Dorothy would remain in Kigali and work in the Free Methodist churches there. Willard, along with his wife and son, who had recently arrived, would move southwest to Kibogora (Key-buh-GORE-uh). "I'll teach school," Willard explained, "and Doris will work as a nurse in the Free Methodist Hospital." They arranged for their son, Sam, to attend school at the mission station.

Dorothy wrote all of this good news to their friends in the United States. She made sure to add, *We appreciate your prayers.*

As time went on, George realized they needed to talk to the Minister of Justice sometime soon. "We must find out exactly what he will require us to do," he explained.

Amminidab said to George a few days later, "I prayed about your government recognition. I also talked to an important official from the office of the

Minister of Justice. He told me that if you go straight to that department first, the officials will say "No" to your request. In that case, you would have almost no chance to ever get recognized."

George sighed. "What should we do?"

"Meet the requirements first," Amminidab answered. "Then talk to the Minister of Justice."

"It sounds like the same old merry-go-round," George said with a sigh.

* * *

On a Friday in September, George and Silas drove to the southeast corner of Kigali to visit the area called Kicukiro (Key-chew-KEY-roo). "I've been thinking more and more that this would be a good place to begin our work," he said. "Many people live here and it's close to a paved road. There's electricity and water, too."

"Yes," Silas answered, "and plenty of property is still available here."

The next Sunday, Silas arrived early. "I have something special to tell you," he said to George.

Chapter 9

MOVING AHEAD

George listened with interest as Silas explained. "Last night while everyone else slept, I prayed. In my mind, God showed me a church in this area. A crowd had gathered there to worship. I saw you and Fergusons, also. I preached, and afterward many people prayed for God to forgive their sins. They asked me about the beliefs of your church, too."

George smiled as he replied, "Silas, I believe God showed you last night that we'll have a Friends Church here. I feel encouraged. We missionaries will have a part in the new church, and you, also, will preach here. Many people will come to Jesus."

Silas shook George's hand as he said heartily, "My wife and I are ready to be part of this new church."

* * *

Early in 1987, George and Dorothy heard disturbing news: "Bishop Aaron has become seriously ill. He may not get well unless the Lord performs a miracle."

"His illness could affect our plans," said George. "We must tell our friends in the United States to pray for the bishop. He's important in his own church as well as to all Christians in Rwanda."

The bishop's illness concerned George and Dorothy. Other situations did, too.

One morning Silas arrived at work with a distressed look on his face. "You know my wife and children have had much sickness recently. Now, her sickness has affected her mind." His voice caught in a sob as he continued. "My wife's afraid I'll kill her. She packed her belongings and went to stay with cousins."

George patted the workman on the shoulder. "I'm sorry, Silas. You had better take time off and try to set the situation right."

At the end of two weeks, Silas came back smiling. "The Lord answered prayer," he reported. "My wife returned home and her fears have gone. She wants to participate in family prayers again."

George shook hands with Silas. "Praise God for answered prayer."

"We have another problem, though," Silas said. "The man who owns the house we live in lost his job. He wants to make our house into a store. We must move immediately."

All at once George had an idea. "Maybe this is the opportunity we have looked for. We've been wanting to make contacts in the Kicukiro area. If

Dorothy in their house in Kigali.

George studying with Silas.

you could move into a big house there, we could use it as a meeting place for worship services."

Silas's face brightened. He clapped his hands in delight. "Yes! Yes, that's what I will look for. It would be wonderful to gather people together for the beginning of our church."

Silas located a suitable house that same day. George looked at it and immediately handed over the first rent payment.

Now and then, news of the bishop's condition reached George and Dorothy. "He's better," some said one day. Not long after, the news changed. "He's worse again and has gone to Belgium for treatment."

"Our hopes of having Bishop Aaron help us have now disappeared," said George. God encouraged him, though, as he read the Bible and prayed. He felt even better the day he and Amminidab received permission to hold services in the house Silas and his family had moved into.

"We will have the first service on May 10," George announced. He built benches and made a church sign. Silas, Amos, and Amminidab visited in the homes located nearby.

Dorothy said, "I don't expect more than 15 people to come for our first service."

As it turned out, forty people crowded into Silas's living room on that first Sunday. The adults sat on one side while the children plopped down on the other. George preached, and afterward nine people came forward to receive Christ as their Savior.

Forty people attended the next Sunday service, seven of them new ones. "We praise God for His blessing," said George that evening. "We're happy that finally we have opportunity to minister. At last we feel like we're moving ahead."

As the new church got under way, the missionaries decided Amminidab would be the pastor. Silas and Amos would help, also.

Each Sunday, some people showed up out of curiosity. Others wanted to be on hand in case new job opportunities appeared. A few had been part of other churches at one time, while others had not. Some of the interested Banyarwanda had never heard the Gospel before. They realized this new church offered spiritual help.

"I have a list of 12 or 13 people who want to become members of our church," Amminidab told George.

"I'm glad to hear that," George replied. "Having members is one of the requirements."

By August, the Sunday morning attendance had increased to eighty. The weekly schedule also included prayer meetings and classes for new converts.

Bishop Aaron returned to Kigali that month. He had not fully recovered, but nevertheless, he met with George and Willard. They told him all that had happened in his absence.

"The best thing I can do for you will be to introduce you to the Minister of Justice," the bishop replied. He then promised to do so soon.

George and Willard once again felt encouraged.

Time passed and delays interfered, one after another. The important introduction to the Minister of Justice did not happen. Meanwhile, another missionary predicted gloomily, "You'll never get the recognition you want from the government."

George replied calmly, "If it's the Lord's will, it will happen. If not, we don't want it anyway."

Enock, a member of the President's Council and also the Minister of Coffee, said to George one day, "I will be glad to speak to the Minister of Justice on behalf of Friends."

George knew Enock well because the Rawsons had introduced them, so he accepted his offer.

Enock reported to George within a few days, saying, "The Minister of Justice thinks you can have the proper recognition from the government."

"That's the best news we've heard yet," George exclaimed. "I feel like God's going to work a miracle."

The day finally arrived for George and Willard to see the Minister of Justice. Bishop Aaron went along and introduced the missionaries to him. "I know these men well," he said. "I attended to their school in Burundi."

"What do you want to say for yourselves?" the minister asked George and Willard.

"We have prepared a statement," replied George, handing him the documents they had organized.

The Minister of Justice read the papers that told about their meeting place and about the people who wanted to become members. After he finished reading, he simply said, "That's it. My assistant will help you from here on."

George and Willard followed the assistant into another room. "The minister didn't even ask questions," George whispered to Willard. "I can't believe it."

"This is a wonderful surprise," Willard replied.

The minister's assistant put the papers on his desk. "You've done a good job," he told the missionaries.

That evening, the Thomases and the Fergusons talked about what had happened that day. They prayed, too. "Lord, please make this miracle happen."

George and Dorothy began to talk about returning to the United States. "Actually, we've accomplished what we came to Rwanda to do," they decided. "Everything's in the hands of the officials from here on."

Before long, they declared, "We plan to leave in September."

George followed a Burundi custom on their final Sunday at the Kicukiro church. He handed a new hoe to Willard. "I give this hoe to you, Willard, to show that I am now giving my jobs to you."

Other church leaders stepped up to place their hands on the hoe, too. "We will all work together," the men said. Everyone rushed forward to say goodbye to George and Dorothy. Many had tears in their eyes.

The Thomases arrived in the United States a few days later. They waited anxiously for news about the miracle in Rwanda.

Hoe Ceremony. Left to right – Amos, Amminidab, Willard, Silas, Nathan (Dorothy's gardener).

Chapter 10

A REASON TO SHOUT

Before George and Dorothy reached Oregon, they received a message. *The mission at Rough Rock needs your help. Please consider going back there for a short time.*

They arrived at their Newberg home a few days later. "We'll go to Rough Rock," they said, and began to repack their belongings.

The shouting-good news came in the midst of their preparations for Arizona. *Our church received government recognition*, stated the message from Willard Ferguson. *The Minister of Justice signed the official papers on October 13. We praise God for His faithfulness, and we thank Him for His answers to prayer.*

George's smile grew wider and wider as he read the message two more times. "I feel like shouting!" he exclaimed.

"Me, too!" answered Dorothy.

"What a miracle," George muttered, shaking his head. "Just think of the churches we've heard about that had to give up their plans. The government in Rwanda wouldn't allow their missionaries to stay."

"Our church has been in Rwanda less than two years," Dorothy replied.

George paced across their bedroom, stepping around a big box of blankets. "I hope our people here realize this isn't any ordinary situation. It's a MIRACLE!"

"Now our congregation there can organize all on their own," said Dorothy, "thanks to the help Bishop Aaron gave us."

"Many others helped, too," said George as he tucked in the flaps of the big brown box. "Our time in Rwanda added up to a good lesson in patience. The delays we thought so unnecessary were all part of God's plan. He knew the right time for everything."

As George and Dorothy headed for Arizona, their friends observed, "They never take time out."

The Thomases spent seven months teaching the Navajo Christians about church membership. During that time, they also supervised the translation of the book, *What We Believe*, from English into Navajo.

"We like what we read in this book," the translator and his wife told George one day. "We want to join the church."

George and Dorothy completed their work on the Indian reservation early the next year. Once again they drove back to their home in Newberg.

Rosemary and Mike, along with their two daughters, lived close by. Becky, her husband, Mark Ankeny, and their two girls would soon move to Newberg.

"It's good to live close to our family again," George and Dorothy said.

As usual, they found plenty to do. George worked at jobs here and there. He and Dorothy had a big garden each summer. Eager for news from the mission field, they prayed that God would continue working miracles.

Then came an unexpected opportunity in December 1990. Maurice Roberts of Mid-America Friends asked George to go along with him as he encouraged Christians in Burundi and Rwanda.

While in Burundi, the men traveled over rough, muddy roads in and out through the mountains. Sometimes they had to push the car, but that did not bother George at all. He delighted in once again being in this wonderful, familiar place.

The Barundi Christians happily welcomed the two visitors. It had been a long time since they had seen missionaries. Several years before, trouble in the land had made it necessary for most missionaries to leave.

"God has helped us in our difficulties," the Christians said. "Our churches have grown."

"I'm glad you've been faithful to God in spite of the troubles," said George.

He delighted in seeing Ndabashinze, by that time gray-haired and nearly blind. The old man greeted his former travel mate with a smile and a firm handshake.

As they visited churches, George preached and also interpreted Maurice's messages into Kirundi. "I've been away from Burundi for 16 years," George said. "Now suddenly I have dropped back into the middle of the Kirundi language." He did well, however, and Maurice said, "George is the right man to have along."

George saw many of the outschools he had built so many years before. He remembered sitting at the top of the rafters, looking out across the hills and valleys. "God has answered my prayers," he said. "Now, many of these areas have newer and larger buildings. They're made with materials more permanent than mud and sticks. And the people still love God. They have worked hard to bring others to Him."

George and Maurice visited in Rwanda next. There, they heard again how God had worked the miracle. The missionaries told about the twelve congregations and two schools that kept them busy. "The church leaders work hard, too," they said. "Several more communities want churches and pastors."

George returned home full of enthusiasm for what he had seen in Burundi and Rwanda. "This trip helped me understand something," he said. "Buildings and people get old and vehicles wear out. But God and His work go on and on."

Praise the Lord —
Amen